MAKO SHARKS

Anne Welsbacher

Capstone Press

MINNEAPOLIS

Printed in the United States of America.

Capstone Press • 2440 Fernbrook Lane • Minneapolis, MN 55447

Editorial Director   John Coughlan
Managing Editor   John Martin
Production Editor   James Stapleton
Copy Editor   Thomas Streissguth

Library of Congress Cataloging-in-Publication Data

Welsbacher, Anne, 1955-
  Mako sharks / by Anne Welsbacher.
    p. cm. -- (Sharks)
   Includes bibliographical references (p.) and index.
   ISBN 1-56065-272-1
   1. Shortfin mako--Juvenile literature. 2. Mako sharks--Juvenile literature. [1. Mako sharks. 2. Sharks.] I. Title. II. Series: Welsbacher, Anne, 1955-   Sharks.
  QL638.95.L3W44 1996
  597'.31--dc20   95-7351
                             CIP
                             AC

99 98 97 96 95   6 5 4 3 2 1